I Keep S

Keep Seeing

11:11

Do You?

An Exploration and Guide for
What to Do Next

NATASHA NANDA

This book is dedicated to

Sheila Rani Bassi

Gone but Not Forgotten.

Our Memories Will Always Keep You Alive
And
Forever In Our Hearts

x

CONTENTS

ABOUT THE AUTHOR

Natasha Nanda was born and raised in Manchester by her father who was an engineer and her spiritual healer mother who was gifted with abilities such as: Channeling, tarot reading, clairvoyancy, empathic and clairsentient. Natasha had many profound spiritual experiences as she was growing up. Clairsentient and empathic, herself, with the help of her mother she learned to understand, harness and control her spiritual side.

After studying at The University of Salford and gaining a Bsc Hons Degree in Paediatric Nursing she joined the NHS but, being altruistic in nature, she was left disheartened by the system. This led to a career change and working on behalf of charity organisations such as: Green Peace UK, Action Aid, Save The Children, Breakthrough Breast Cancer, World Vision and many more. An opportunity to work in Australia came up and she worked for a Cancer Charity in Adelaide, Melbourne and Sydney.

Yearning for something more Natasha left her job to go backpacking around Thailand and Australia for several months. Working in small villages, teaching English, opened her eyes to different religions, beliefs, circumstances and cultures. This, combined with meditation, helped her open up spiritually and by becoming more attuned to her surroundings she gained a level of insight, knowledge and wisdom about herself and those around her.

The breakdown of her family, losing a friend to a tragic accident, losing contact with her mother, sexual harassment and discrimination in the work place, health issues and domestic violence, which almost cost her life, all over a relatively short span of time caused Natasha's life to spiral downwards. This led to stress, anxiety, depression, drug and alcohol misuse and an attempt to take her own life by overdose.

Thankfully she survived, and this and all her experiences were a wake-up call. Natasha turned to God, self-help books, and meditation to turn her life around. This was when she began experiencing seeing 11:11 more prominently. Through communicating with Divine Spirits she was led to find her first and one true love, who she later married and had a baby with. The number sequences led her on a journey where she was able to turn her life around for the better.

Now settled down, happy and content Natasha wanted to help others. She began by setting up social media platforms relating to 11:11 and inviting people to email her about it. Thousands of testimonials of peoples experiences and insights into 11:11 followed. This is where she gained a deeper insight into the phenomenon. She began researching and asking questions in order to write a book that could provide answers and help others understand their experiences with 11:11.

Natasha's research and understanding of 11:11 and her spirituality combined with her personal life experiences has enabled her to help others and contributed to her mission, which is to unite and guide other people in their 11:11 experience, not to fear it but to embrace it.

To learn more about the Author and her life please refer to her website:

www.Ikeepseeing1111.com

INTRODUCTION

I kept seeing 11:11 everywhere and it was beginning to drive me crazy. It felt as though these numbers were stalking me. Every time I glanced somewhere it was right there, staring me in the face.

At first I would glance at the time and it would be 11:11 or 1:11 am/pm. This happened often. It was a random occurrence and I promise you I was not clock watching! However it wasn't just on the time. It had a strange tendency to pop up unexpectedly in the most interesting and unique ways imaginable.

For example, I would be in the kitchen cooking and I'd randomly stop the microwave at 1 minute and 11 seconds. I would pick up the remote control to pause the TV to get a drink and I would see 1 hour 11 minutes frozen on the screen. When walking down the street a business van would drive past and the telephone number ended in 1111. Whilst reading a text message I would notice it was sent at 11:11am. Even when I was purchasing a few products on the internet, the bill would accumulate to £11.11!

It did not stop there though. I was seeing 11:11 and other number sequences such as 1:11, 111 and 1111 literally everywhere you could think of. Have any of these things ever happened to you or someone you know? Perhaps you notice these sequences in other places such as:

Oven timers
Road signs
License plates
Sat Nav guides
Parking bays
Car mileage counters
Ticket numbers
Bills
ID badges
Social Media sites
Game scores

Maybe your birthday is on the 11th November? Could it be that this specific date, number or time has some significance or meaning to you? Either way, the list of these sightings and experiences are endless.

What are the chances of this happening as a daily occurrence? Do you ever wonder or ask yourself, *"What's all this about and what does it mean?"* I know I have on many occasions! If the answer is '*Yes*' to any of the questions I have posed so far, then your eyes are in the right place.

If you are experiencing this, cast your mind back to when you first started to experience it. How did it make you **feel**?

When I first started to experience seeing 11:11 regularly I would:

Gasp for air in shock, disbelief and amazement.

My heart would skip a beat.

It would send shivers up my spine and goose pimples down my arm.

It was not only affecting me physically but also mentally. It made me feel an array of emotions:

Unnerved

Scared

Uncomfortable

Anxious

Perplexed

Freaked out

What did you **think** when you first started to see these numbers frequently? What thoughts were running through your mind?

When I first started to see 11:11 over and over again I used to think or say, *"What are the chances of that? There it is again 111... It must be a coincidence..."* With time it became much more intense and I would continue to say to myself, *"Oh No, not again! What's all this 11:11 business about?"* It even began to annoy and frustrate me.

Yes, 11:11 was now stirring up a whirlwind in my mind. All of these thoughts, feelings and questions were whizzing around uncontrollably at 111 mph. Maybe you too feel or have felt like this before?

Do you interpret seeing 11:11 as *'just a coincidence'?* Maybe it is! But what if it's not? What if, there is more to seeing 11:11 than meets the eye?

Think of the mathematical probability of this occurrence being put down solely to chance? Have you thought about that? I know I have and I must admit my maths are not great but what I was experiencing was in fact defying coincidence and chance, so obviously there was more to it.

I needed answers and I had two burning questions.

"What does 11:11 mean and what do I do now?"

After many years of seeing these number sequences and searching, I became confused with all the information out there. It was like a minefield and the whirlwind was now picking up speed to 1,111 mph. I needed to tame this storm in my mind and that was when I decided to embark on my own personal journey into discovering its meaning.

I spent many years journaling, researching and speaking to other people who were experiencing these occurrences, in great depth. With all my knowledge, insights and resources, I experimented with various methods to understand why 11:11 was so persistent in getting my attention. After researching and conversing with many people who were in my situation, I can now attempt to answer those questions and share them with the world.

The purpose of this book is to guide you down many different avenues to consider and think about. It is an exploration of information, facts, personal stories, techniques, strategies and methods to further your knowledge and awareness.

Because the 11:11 concept may be difficult to grasp and digest, I have purposely sectioned this book into three main areas, which can be seen within the contents page.

All the chapters are short and simple so that you may use it as a tool book and refer to it when needed.

I hope that I can guide you on your journey into understanding what 11:11 means to you, by inviting you to read on.

So, let the journey of 11:11 begin, with each turn of our page.

> *"The eye only sees what the mind is*
> *prepared to comprehend."*
> **Henri Bergson**

"You are the one. That is why you see The Ones. But you are not the only one who sees The Ones. But if all those ones that see The Ones unite together as one, with one main goal to make a difference, then The Ones would have served their purpose". **Natasha Nanda**

PART ONE

Exploration into 11:11 - What Is 11:11 All About?

"I am learning to trust the journey, even when I don't understand it."

Mila Bron

1

Who Sees 11:11?

Do you ever think or feel like you are going crazy? Well if you are, so are millions of other people. Yes, millions! Seeing 11:11 is a global phenomenon that appears to be taking the world by a storm. People from all walks of life around the world are experiencing this occurrence. If you don't believe me, Google it. You will be shocked at what you discover!

Yes, there are discussion groups on Facebook with Statuses reading:

"I wake up at exactly 1:11 am at night."
"I see 1111 in my dreams."
"What does 11:11 mean? I have been seeing it for years."
"I see 11:11,1:11,111,1111 everywhere."

People on Twitter, Tweeting:

"I keep seeing 11:11?"
"11:11 Make a wish"
"@ikeepseeing1111 Why do I keep seeing 11:11?"
"#11:11".

Pictures of people's sightings have inundated our social media networks and the amount of '11:11' screenshots captured are unbelievable. Have you ever screen shot such happenings yourself? Maybe you have hundreds of pictures stored on your mobile phone? I know I have!

But, it doesn't stop at these! There's also vast amounts of blogs, websites, YouTube clips and radio shows dedicated to this particular subject. The wealth of knowledge, information and people who are experiencing this is truly mind blowing. Even famous people are sharing personal experiences and insights into this topic.

Talk show host Ellen DeGeneres named her record label 'eleven-eleven' saying; *"Everytime I look at the clock, it's 11:11. Whenever I'm anywhere, I see 1111 all the time."*
https://en.m.wikipedia.org/wiki/Eleveneleven

Then there's, Boston Indie Rock band *"Come"*, who had a debut album which was entitled *11:11*. The members of the band decided on this title after glancing at a digital clock on several occasions and finding it was 11:11 each time. Brokaw (a band member) said that *"It was a recurring phenomenon, it became a sort of superstitious mantra."*

https://en.m.wikipedia.org/wiki/11:11_(Come_album)

Even Uri Gellar describes how he first began seeing 11:11 when he was forty years old. He said, *"At first I thought they were coincidences. I would stand with my back to a digital clock and something made me turn around and I would notice that the time would be 11:11. These incidents intensified. I would be checked into hotel rooms on floor 11 room 1111. I started noticing these digits on computers, microwave ovens, cars, documents, etc. I decided to write about it on my website. I was immediately inundated by hundreds of emails from all around the world. Individuals were telling me their own 11:11 stories, almost always saying "I thought it only happened to me".*

http://www.urigeller.com/articles/11.htm

Not only were people seeing it, others such as Austin Mahone, an American pop singer, entitled his self-released single "11:11" to iTunes. It is renowned as the "Make a Wish" song, which went viral.

Yes! This phenomenon is very much real and is not a figment of the imagination. The fact that 11:11 has even made it into *Wikipedia* (the biggest online encyclopaedia), demonstrates the scale and volume of this very subject. What a relief it must be, to know that there are others who share this experience.

You can now safely take a deep breath in, exhale, relax and take comfort from the knowledge that you are not alone. And, you're definitely not going mad! Clearly something big is going on, but do you ever wonder what it's all about?

2

Is it a Coincidence?

At first when we start to see 11:11 we may think, *"What a coincidence." "Oh, there it is again?"* We may dismiss it as *'strange'*, just *'pure chance'* or *'luck?'* Then we continue with what we were doing, without giving it much thought. But, as time passes by, the 11:11 we see so often begins to intensify in frequency.

Yes, now we begin to see it almost everyday, sometimes several times a day. Perhaps even *'freaking'* us out when it catches us off guard? We may even question the very essence of this bizarre sighting. Is it really just a coincidence or is there an underlying reason, one that delves much deeper than we originally thought?

Well, some sceptics believe that seeing 11:11 is nothing more than a mere *'coincidence'*. But, how does a sceptic's explanation apply when, for example: We open a book randomly at page 111? A car drives in front of us with a license plate reading 1111? Our food bill total amounts to £111.11?

It's haunting presence cannot be escaped. Has this ever happened to you? Coincidence, you tell yourself, or is it?

Think about it. What are the chances of these occurrences happening in one day, almost everyday? For some it happens for weeks, months and even years on end. If they are not coincidences, then what are they?

Carl Jung, a Swiss psychologist explains such happenings. He proposed the idea that when several meaningful occurrences happen, it is *not* a coincidence. It is, *"the occurrence of two or more events that appear to be meaningfully related but not causally related"*. His integration of spirituality and psychology helped him come to a conclusion that external events guide us towards greater self-awareness. He coined this term as *"synchronicity"* as opposed to a coincidence, whereby synchronicity is considered to be more of a *"meaningful coincidence"*.

The word *'synchronicity'* itself, derives from the Greek word *"chronos"* which means time. How apt is that, when seeing 11:11, especially on the time? New age author and senior scientist, Deepak Chopra elaborates on this term; *"Synchronicity means 'in time'. Meaningful coincidences which present opportunities all around us."* In his book, *SynchroDestiny: Harnessing the infinite power of coincidence to create miracles,* he proposes two things.

1. *That we can dismiss these as random occurrences.*
2. *Recognise them as a potentially life altering event.*

He believes that every coincidence is a message and a clue about a particular facet of our lives that requires our attention. He goes on to explain, *"By paying attention to life's coincidences, you can learn to hear their messages more clearly".*

It seems that we're a part of something much bigger and something is trying to communicate with us by attempting to get our attention. But who or what is it?

3

Who or What is it?

Synchronistic experiences such as seeing 11:11 can be viewed as messages, but from whom?

The source of 11:11 has been described by many who experience this occurrence, as a Divine presence much greater than themselves. Although not always seen by the eye they may be sensed or heard in our thoughts and hearts. These *Spirit Guides, Divine Beings* and *Entities* can be depicted as:

- God
- The Universe
- Angels
- A loved one who has passed away
- Guiding Stars
- Guardian Spirits

Whatever it may be, I will refer to them as "Spirit Guides" throughout this book.

Most people have their own Spirit Guide, which they believe in. Some believe in one, but others may believe in many. Do you believe in any of these or maybe something else? Could these be the force behind our 11:11 experience?

For me personally, I believe that the force behind 11:11 are Angels. I remember having a conversation about this with my friend. I told her how I believed in Angels and how I felt it was them that were communicating to me via 11:11.

You may be laughing right now and saying, *"Ha ha! There's no such thing as Angels!"* Well, that is okay because that is exactly what my Friend said. Yes, she responded to this by laughing at me, looking at me like I was mad and mocking me for my beliefs. Once she had finished, I thanked her for her point of view and said;

"Can I change the subject and ask you a question?"

"Yes," she replied, unaware that I was *not* actually changing the topic.

"Do you believe in God?"

"Yes." She answered.

"Why do you believe in God?"

"Because when I pray to him I know he is there and that he is listening to me. I know that he will answer my prayers."

"So you believe in God?" I replied, with a confused expression.

"You believe in a God because he answers your prayers, he listens to you, BUT... you have NEVER seen him?"

My friend stopped to think and reluctantly replied, *"Yes."*

"Well I believe in Angels. I talk to them and pray to them. They listen to me, answer my prayers and questions in the form of the number 11:11. I too have never seen them. I just know they are with me, just like you. So why do you ridicule and mock me for my beliefs, when you too have never seen God?"

My friend was left shocked, confused and speechless to my response.

The point that I am trying to make is, our Spirit Guide can be anything we believe it to be. There is no right or wrong to it, it's what comforts us and makes us happy. A belief is personal to you, just like your journey with 11:11 is unique and personal to you.

Some individuals may not believe in any of them and feel it to be a negative force. If so, maybe those negative feelings arise through fear of the unknown or not understanding it? Perhaps we are just too used to our everyday routine, that we do not want to step outside our comfort zone to find out. Fear of the unknown can prohibit our learning and with that our potential growth. Hopefully, I can shed some light throughout this book and show you a positive side to what 11:11 can bring.

Either way, perhaps we all have Spirit Guides assigned to us? If so, could it be that their job is to present opportunities to us, to help assist us in our lives. Making sure we meet the right people and arrange the right *'coincidences'* (synchronistic moments) for us? They are all possibilities if only we are open to them. After all, we can't change things in our head if we're not aware of them.

If we become an observer of our thoughts and become a self-examiner when we see 11:11, we are more likely to do something about it. And clearly you are, as you are reading this book!

However, the next question we may ask ourselves is "why me?" Yes, why are these Spirit Guides trying to contact us?

4

Why Me?

People begin to see 11:11 at different points in their life. Many people have been seeing it for years, others may have just started to notice it. And some, don't notice it at all. But why?

On researching and conversing with those who are experiencing the 11:11 phenomenon, I found several common themes running through their experiences.

People report seeing 11:11 when going through significant life changes, feelings or obstacles. Let's explore a few of these:

A desire to break free: To find purpose, direction or the meaning to life.

Embarking on new things: Setting up a new business, moving locations, going travelling, new job, career or relationships.

Health issues: Disease or illness such as Cancer, stress, anxiety or depression.

Drug abuse: Taking substances like cannabis, cocaine, heroin, ecstasy or alcohol to pacify the problems and pain experienced.

Death: Losing a loved one through illness, tragic accidents or murder. Thus creating a variety of emotions such as grief, pain and anger.

Abuse: Sexual, physical, emotional and psychological abuse. Under this umbrella fall many scenarios: child abuse, rape, assault, self-harm, bullying and domestic violence.

Relationship issues: Partners breaking trust, arguments, becoming more distant, change in beliefs.

Financial hardship: Struggling to pay bills, rent, mortgages. Not having enough money to buy food.

Cast your mind back to when you first started to see 11:11. Were you going through any of these changes? If so, perhaps 11:11 was reaching out to you when you needed guidance or direction in your life?

There are also, other possible explanations worth exploring too. For instance, my partner is sometimes with me when I see 11:11/111/1111 and I tend to point it out to him by saying, *"Oh look, 1111 the Angels are with me"*.

I always questioned, *"Why do I always notice these numbers, but he doesn't? Why me?"* Do you ever wonder why this happens, especially when that person is stood right next to you?

It could be a difference in perception and awareness, in that everyone notices things at different times. Let's think about this by using a traffic accident as an illustration:

After a car crash, police ask for witnesses to come forward and describe what happened. They like to have as many witness statements as possible so that they can build up enough evidence to give them a broader, more realistic version of events.

There will be many *different* perspectives on what happened. The driver of one car will have one perception, other drivers or passengers will have yet another. Each onlooker who witnessed the accident will have a slightly different perspective, depending on where they were, how far they were, how good a view they had and what else was going on. Maybe they were not looking? Perhaps they were asleep or doing something else like, reading or using their phone?

It's the same principle with 11:11. Each situation, experience, event and conversation, means something different to all those involved and also to those not involved. We attach different meanings, according to our belief systems, how we are affected by the experience and how much attention we were paying to it. Maybe other people are not paying attention when 11:11 makes an appearance? Perhaps their thoughts and eyes are somewhere different to yours?

Think about it. There are so many signs around us, all we have to do is look up and notice them. However, many people do not look up. They are too busy looking down. People are so consumed by what they are doing or are distracted they miss out on possible opportunities, signs and messages that are being conveyed to them. Too busy, they don't pay attention to the wonders and possibilities that surround them.

Could this be the reason why we are starting to see these numbers embedded within technology more frequently? Are we all guilty to some extent of being consumed with technology or being too busy? I know I am! Perhaps this is why we see 11:11 within technology and it is waking us up to come away from such things? It's worth considering surely. Who knows, maybe it is part of our destiny and it is our Spirit Guides, orchestrating this Divine gift to help us on our journeys?

These are just a few examples. Perhaps the reason we see 11:11 will unfold for us to understand at some point in our lives? Maybe when things are clearer or with time? Could it be that 11:11 is guiding us towards the next phase or chapter in our lives?

Rather than focusing for too long on why it is happening to us or how we see these number sequences, we could try diverting our attention to what it could mean and what it presages. Maybe we will later discover the reason *"Why me"* if we haven't already done so?

5

What Does 11:11 Mean?

The predominant question surrounding the 11:11 occurrence, which millions of people are experiencing, is the million dollar question. A question that many people are searching for the answers and asking.

"What does 11:11 mean?"

As an author, I would love to give you a definitive answer. However, the truth is there is no conclusive or universal definition. (Please don't shoot me down just yet. Let me finish explaining before you tut, sigh or role your eyes in disappointment).

As frustrating as this revelation may be, the reason why there is no universal definition, is simply because the 11:11 phenomenon is an experience. Let me clarify this using an example, in terms of a finger print.

Each persons fingerprint is unique to each individual. No print is ever the same, just like no journey is ever the same.

Therefore, the interpretations of 11:11 is subject to the interpreter, the interpreter being us. What it may mean to you or me, may be different to what it means to *Jack* or *Jill* down the road.

You see, many things have multiple meanings, just like 11:11 can have many different meanings. Take for instance the English language as an example, almost every word in the Dictionary has a multiple meaning. Look at the word *"date"* in the dictionary:

Date - *her favourite fruit is a date/ Jack took Jill out on a date/ I will book that date in my diary.*

As you can see, the word *'Date'* has several meanings. But, it depends on the context in which it is used, that makes the meaning understandable. This is how 11:11 is. If there was a dictionary for numbers there would be many meanings embedded within it. You would put them into the context of your situation and journey, in order for it to make sense to you.

Do not be deflated when I say there is no set definition of 11:11. That does not mean that there is no meaning! As much as I would love to serve you a definition onto a plate, I am afraid I can't, nor can anyone else. It just means you have to discover the meaning for yourself. It is what resonates with you, that is where the meaning lays.

But what we can do, is explore several explanations and theories that surround 11:11, that may contribute to discovering the meaning behind it. It's like a jigsaw puzzle, we're slowly connecting all the pieces, before we can see the bigger picture. So, let's continue connecting those pieces together...

6

What are the Theories and Explanations Surrounding 11:11?

Remember in the introduction, when I talked about that minefield of information that spun me around at 1,111 mph? Well brace yourselves, we are about to embark in that area, in this chapter.

You may have already researched some of them in great depth and know most of this. If so, feel free to skim read or skip this section. If you haven't, maybe it will give you something to think about and who knows where it may lead you?

I won't lie to you, it can be a lot of information to digest and may cause some degree of confusion. I want to pre-empt this, so you do not curse me for this minefield you are about to step into. This is because there's no universal meaning.

Hopefully, you will find a definition that has meaning to you, within the context of your life and belief system. If not, do not worry I have more things to help aid you to discover it, within Part 2 of this book.

This chapter is here to fuel your mind with all this information, to do what you will with it. If that means throwing it in the garbage bin, so be it. (At this point I would suggest to grab yourself a drink, this part may cause you to experience some level of turbulence. Don't say I didn't warn you!)

So without further ado, put your seatbelt on and let's continue. Take a deep breath, absorb what you want and discard the rest, we are about to travel through that minefield and remember...

"Everyone in a complex system has a slightly different interpretation. The more interpretations we gather, the easier it becomes to gain a sense of the whole." Margaret J Wheatley.

God

Do you believe in God? Could 11:11 be embedded within the language of God?

Living in a world of numbers, where verbal communication is being diminished this could have been foreseen by Him. Technology such as mobile phones, computers, laptops and Ipads dominate this century. Instead of communicating verbally we are tapping buttons and sending emails and text messages instead.

Is talking face to face or over the phone, slowly fading away? Is this the reason why numbers may have been chosen by God, as a trigger to wake us up? To follow our hearts that contain the voice of God, because He knew this would happen? After all He sees the overall scheme of things and is considered to be all knowing and seeing.

People who believe in God, express how He can communicate in many different ways. This is ingrained in many religious and philosophical texts. Let's look at a few examples of how God may communicate:

- Tongues
- Being able to recite religious texts
- Hearing God's words
- Feeling and sensing God's presence
- Visions
- Dreams
- Signs

People believe that He speaks through many avenues and we are to seek His voice. If this is the case, then is it possible that He uses meaningful coincidences, even numbers to get our attention? Always bringing us back to Him and remaining at the centre of it all?

People have claimed that God has given them messages, through 11:11 to seek out texts in religious/other books. They have felt guided and pushed to seek such pages. For example, in the Bible, through Jesus Christ 1111 has been suggested to equate and represent:

1 mind
1 body
1 spirit
1 accord

For example, verses within the bible state:

- (*Philippians 2:2*) *Fulfill ye my joy, that ye be likeminded, having the same love, being of one accord, of one mind.*

- (*Ephesians 4:4*) *There is one body, and one Spirit, even as ye are called in one hope of your calling;*

- (*1 Corinthians 12:12*) *For as the body is one, and hath many members, and all the members of that one body, being many, are one body: so also is Christ.*

However, it is not just in Christianity. Scriptures from Judaism, Islam, Hinduism and Buddhism are only but a few examples where oneness occurs. Although all these religions have different concepts and ideologies, there appears to be one fundamental thing they have in common. This is to, *"love thy neighbour."*

Is oneness about love? Loving everyone and uniting as one to make us whole? If we put religion to one side and all have a new religion which is love, would the world not have one common purpose, regardless of difference?

Is God communicating to us in the form of 11:11? Could this be a direct line to God, whereby He is using 11:11 to prompt and remind us of His presence? If so, maybe we could pray for guidance when we see such numbers.

Angels

Do you ever feel like a loved one who has crossed over is with you? Trying to communicate with you? Maybe you believe, saw, sensed or spoken to Angels?

Many people believe that 11:11 is directly related to Angels, guiding us on a daily basis. *Doreen Virtue Ph.D* is a successful author, who has published over 50 books, Angel therapy being her field of expertise. Her bestselling book is titled: *"Angel Numbers 101: The meaning of 111, 123, 444 and Other Number Sequences."*

She proposes, we all have Guardian Angels and a common way they communicate, is by showing repetitive number sequences. Her explanation of what the Angels say, are:-

"We can't write our messages to you in the sky. You've got to pay attention and believe when you see any patterns forming in your life — especially in response to any questions or prayers you've posed. When you hear the same song repeatedly or see the same number sequence, who do you think is behind this? Your angels, of course!"

The book is like a dictionary for numbers which interprets and explains the significance of 1111 and what to do. She is an author that is recommended when searching for knowledge within this particular area.

Could it be that Angels are trying to connect with us through 11:11? Could this be a loved one who has passed away? Perhaps you have had signs that confirm such an existence. Whatever it maybe, it's what resonates with you.

Numerology

Do you believe in Numerology? That every number has a meaning and that it plays a role in one's destiny?

Numerology is any belief in Divine, mystical or other special relationships between a number and any coinciding events.

St. Augustine of Hippo (A.D. 354–430) wrote, *"Numbers are the Universal language offered by the deity to humans as confirmation of the truth."*

This notion is very similar to that of Pythagoras, who also believed that everything had numerical relationships. That it was up to the mind to seek and investigate the secrets of these relationships or have them revealed by Divine Spirits.

Many also claim that seeing 11:11 on a clock is an auspicious sign. Others feel that 11:11 signals a spirit presence. The belief that the time prompt 11:11 has mystical powers has also been adopted by believers in New Age philosophies. It has also been said, that it presents an opportunity to reflect on our purpose for being here. That it is a call to return to balance, to pay attention and to claim our power by mastering the life lessons before us.

Within numerology 11 is considered to be a Master Number. It represents transformation, intuition, creativity, genius, refinement and fulfilment. Numerology enthusiasts and practitioners have always been especially excited about Master Numbers because, as the name implies, they represent something above and beyond the mundane.

Is 11:11 a powerful and spiritual number that illuminates one's path? Perhaps 11:11 is working to awaken us, to express these qualities in our own lives?

The Sixth Month Strategy-Edgar Cayce

Edgar Cayce was born in 1877. He was one of the most compelling person in metaphysics. For more than forty years, the *'Sleeping Prophet'* (as he was sometimes referred to), closed his eyes and entered into an altered state of consciousness. He spoke about subjects such as healing, dreams, prophecy and meditation. He was well known for many things including, his psychic abilities.

In one of his readings he mentioned 11:11. However, this has gone relatively unnoticed until now. In Edgar's reading, 900-429, he stated:

"The first lesson for six months should be One-One-One-One; Oneness of God, oneness of man's relation, oneness of force, oneness of time, oneness of purpose, Oneness in every effort – Oneness – Oneness!"

Could it be that this 11:11 phenomenon was happening before technology existed? That there is something on a much grander scale going on? If Edgar Cayce's reading did coincide with the 11:11 phenomenon of today, then maybe his 6 month strategy is seriously worth considering?

Make a Wish and The Law of Attraction

Have you ever:

- Made a wish whilst blowing out your birthday candles?
- Thrown a coin into a fountain or wishing well and made a wish?
- Made a wish when seeing a shooting star?
- Pulled a wish bone from the Xmas Turkey and made a wish?
- Prayed for your wish to be granted?
- Crossed your fingers in the hope that your wish comes true?

Think about it. What do you do when you make a wish? Do you close your eyes? Think about something you really want with all your heart? Wish whole heartedly that it will come true and then let it go, with the hope that it will come true? Have you ever done any of these things? Is making a wish just a fairy tale programmed into us from a young age? What if there is more to it than meets the eye?

The truth is at some point in our lives we have all closed our eyes, looked deep within ourselves and wished for a certain something. There are various methods of wishing. One of many, is the *"11:11 make a wish"* theory. You may have heard about it from a child, friend or a relative? Maybe you have seen it on social media sites such as Facebook or Pinterest? Twitter feeds are inundated with People tweeting, *"11:11 make a wish"*. Celebrities such as Paris Hilton, also tweet such things. But what does it all mean?

I was driving my car and my ten year old niece pointed at the clock and said, **"Look 11:11 make a wish".**

I asked her what she meant by it and she replied, **"When you see 11:11 you have to make a wish."**

"And, does your wish ever come true?" I asked.

"Yes, some of my wishes have come true." She replied.

Is this just child's play? Maybe you're curious to know more? Let's explore this further:

The act of wishing is: *"The expression of some desire or mental inclination-to make a wish."* Collins Dictionary.

This definition is very similar to the law of attraction, a New Age belief based on the concept that, *'like attracts like'*. The notion is that when we focus upon positive thoughts, we will subsequently manifest them into our lives. In other words what we think and believe we will receive. Our thoughts can also be described in terms of a magnet. Positive thoughts will attract positive things and negative thoughts will attract negative things.

Making a wish and the law of attraction, both share similar meanings but have different names. However, the law of attraction goes into much more depth on how to make those dreams and wishes a reality by doing the following:

1. ASK for what you want.
2. BELIEVE whole heartedly that you already have what you want and desire.
3. RECEIVE it and be grateful that your request was granted.

If we integrate the *"11:11 make a wish"* theory with *"the law of attraction"*, could we manifest our deepest desires into form? Could the Universe, God, Angels or whomever we pray to or ask, grant our wishes if we truly believe, with all our hearts? Maybe there is some truth behind it?

Many also believe that when 11:11 is seen, a doorway of opportunity opens up for one to enter. This is very similar to making a wish when seeing 11:11. It is like a Gateway to our higher consciousness. This Gateway being the mind, whereby our thoughts have the opportunity to move into a more powerful place when 11:11 is present.

It works as a reminder to create our own realities with our thoughts, beliefs, intentions and actions. The message being to choose our thoughts wisely, ensuring that they match our true desires.

Whenever 11:11 presents itself, it is considered to act as a daily reminder to take that one minute to hold our dreams in our hearts and believe in it. To acknowledge the support available from our Spirit Guides and to have the courage to affirm willingness to move. If this is done it is said that we hold the power in our minds to manifest anything that we truly desire.

Does 11:11 have a direct line with our thoughts? Could it be used as a guide to help us manifest our desires? Maybe this is worth considering? If you ever stop and make a wish when you see 11:11, perhaps you could use the law of attraction and make a wish theory and see where it takes you?

DNA Map

The brain can be described as a computer, which relies on binary codes such as 1's and 0's. In this example, 11:11 is considered to be the binary code within our minds. It is like a DNA Map of our inner selves and our thought processes. The number 11 can be seen to represent twin strands of our DNA. With the notion of it being a sign of a DNA activation. Once 11:11 is present in our lives, it activates a part of us that triggers an awakening process.

Is 11:11 triggering our DNA to wake up? Could it be a digital time code? This theory is that, 11:11 unlocks our DNA and opens our subconscious mind through physically seeing these numbers, encouraging our brains to remember the importance of it.

Do you feel like 11:11 has some significance and is important in your life? Do you feel like 11:11 is waking you up to something? Maybe to do a specific thing? If so, do you think it would be a good idea to act upon those intentions?

Fibonacci Sequence and the Golden Ratio

The theory is that, 11:11 is tied into sacred geometry and the Golden Ratio of creation. The Golden Ratio is based upon the Fibonacci sequence which is:

1,1,2,3,5,8,13,21,34,55,89,144,233,377...

If we add the first number in front of the other, the amount equals to the digit next to it and so on. For example:

1+1=2

1+2=3

2+3=5

3+5=8

5+8=13

8+13=21

13+21=34

21+34=55

34+55=89

55+89=144

89+144=233

144+233=377

As you can see it all begins with the number 1. This sequence which is based upon the Golden Ratio, is an irrational number of approximately 1.618033988749 (referred to as "phi"). This ratio is found throughout the natural, scientific and man-made world, as the highest expression of symmetry and balance. Both of which imply a higher order in underlying structures to reality, both in the seen and unseen world.

The Fibonacci numbers and golden ratio are nature's numbering system. They appear almost everywhere in nature, from the leaf arrangement in plants, to the pattern of the florets of a flower. Here are a few examples of where they are considered to appear:

- *Sacred Icons* - The Five Pointed Star, Pentagrams, Swastika, Flower of Life, Crop Circle Images.

- *Architecture* - Greek Temple of Parthenon Athens, Eden Project Plymouth, United Nations building New York, Great Mosque of Kairouan, Notre Dame de Paris

- *Art* - Leonardo da Vinci's famous Vitruvian Man, annunciation, Madonnas with Child and Saints. Michelangelo, the ceiling in the Sistine Chapel.

- *Music* - Stuart Mitchell decoding Roslyn Chapel. The nursery rhyme, Twinkle, Twinkle. Beethoven's Fifth Symphony, Bach.

- *Human Body* - Outstretched arms and legs, Cochlea of the ear, Clenched fists, Face.

- *Nature* - Seeds, Pine Cones, Petals, Fruit, Vegetables, Animals.

The Fibonacci numbers are therefore applicable to the growth of every living thing and even all of mankind. Here numbers are ingrained in the very being of life itself. Therefore, implying that numbers play an important role here on earth.

Does this demonstrate the role numbers play in our lives? Is there more to these numbers? Especially if they are embedded within objects, buildings and nature itself? Maybe even within our consciousness? Does this not show the significance that numbers play in our lives? Take a look for yourselves by doing a *'Google Image search'* of *'Fibonacci sequences'*. You will be amazed by where they appear!

Global Consciousness

Global Consciousness is the notion that when large groups of people unite collectively and focus their minds on the same thing, they influence the world at large.

Raising our consciousness means we focus on our similarities instead of our differences. We don't have to all live in the same way or even within the same system. Maybe we just need to adopt some unifying ideas? For example, kindness, acceptance, compassion and love, whereby we can be the best versions of ourselves. When we feel fear, hate, judgement and apathy we are allowing ourselves to be divided and controlled.

Is it up to each of us to educate ourselves, so we can bring the light of awareness to everything we read, watch and hear? To take responsibility for how we think, feel and act, so we can rise above the old paradigm and look at the world with fresh eyes. Maybe everyone who experiences the 11:11 phenomenon needs to unite together as one, for greater changes to occur?

Could it be that 11:11 is collectively waking up our inner beings, to a world we did not see before? If collectively we see 11:11 could we use it to raise the consciousness of mankind? And, with that make a difference in the evolution process?

Perhaps all we need to do, is connect and unite with other people who are experiencing this. Could this be something worth doing at some point? If so, the last chapter of this book may benefit you.

Lightworkers

Do you have a strong desire to help humanity? Have

you ever felt like you have an important mission? Maybe you do, but don't know what? Could you be a Lightworker, here to shine your light into the world?

Lightworkers are known as Human Angels. They fall under an umbrella of categories: Indigo, crystal, Rainbow and Starseed children. It is believed that they came to assist earth with the next stage in evolution, each of them here for a sacred purpose.

It is said that when Lightworkers stray from their life purpose, they sometimes have a tendency to feel lost and afraid. They know something important is missing in their lives, but are unsure of what. All they know is, they have a strong urge to help humanity. Do you ever feel like this?

All over the world people are awakening and are hearing an inner calling that can no longer be ignored. This call being a reminder that it's time to stop and take steps in finding their purpose. Many are also discovering innate spiritual gifts such as:

- Clairvoyance- clear seeing, or psychic vision
- Clairaudience- clear hearing, or psychic hearing
- Clairsentience- clear feeling/sensing or psychic feeling
- Clairtangency- clear touching

- Claircognizance- clear knowing or psychic knowing
- Clairgustance- clear tasting or psychic tasting
- Clairsentience- clear smelling or psychic smelling

Do you feel like you fall under any of these categories? If so, perhaps you can look further into these gifts.

Maybe 11:11 has something to do with leading humanity into a higher collective consciousness of love and light? If so, then the world is depending on many of these Lightworkers.

Other Explanations

Obviously there are many different theories and explanations that surround 11:11. So here is a list of other possible interpretations for you to look into at your own leisure:

- Twin Flames
- Spiritual Awakening
- Spiritual Sensitivity
- Universal Code
- World Connection
- Activation Code
- Spirit Guardians
- A New Awareness

***

Congratulations, you can breathe out with a sigh of relief, if you managed to read all of those theories. You successfully came through the minefield intact! Maybe slightly disorientated, confused and mind boggled. But, hopefully I can attempt to iron those feelings out, within the next few chapters.

Unfortunately, I had to offer you all the main theories that surround 11:11. This is so that you have a foundation of knowledge that surrounds this phenomenon. After all, broadening your horizons can be a good thing!

Perhaps you would like to take a break from reading if your mind is feeling a little frazzled right now. I understand completely as I have been there! If you do maybe you could think about the following:

When taking all of these explanations into consideration, do any of them resonate with you? Do you feel drawn or connected to any of them? If so, maybe you could explore them in more detail and see where synchronicity takes you. After all this is your journey, I am only here to act as a guide to usher you down potential avenues. Only you can find the answers and decipher it's meaning for yourself.

Remember, this book is specifically here to make you think, ask yourself questions and to guide you in that process. And trust me, there are lots more thought provoking things yet to come. So go on take a break, I wouldn't want your brain to fall out because I gave you too much to think about!

7

What is the Significance of it?

Now that we know there is no definitive meaning, we must continue to ask questions and search, until we find the answers that we are content with. I won't lie, the answers that we are seeking don't always come as a flash of a lightbulb. Although if they did, that would certainly make our lives much easier. I suppose if life was easy, we would not learn or understand anything.

However, let me shine some light onto this subject. There does appear to be a broad significance surrounding 11:11. Many describe it as, a form of *"Wake Up Call"*. The Cambridge Dictionary defines a 'Wake Up Call' as: *"Something that happens...It should make you realise that you need to take action to change a situation."*

When taking this definition and dissecting it, could the *"Something that happens"*, be attributed to seeing the number sequences? Could the *"action"* that needs to be taken be, searching, finding or seeking what it means or what it is communicating to us? If so, then Part 2 of this book will be highly beneficial.

Either way if 11:11 signifies a wake up call, then this is very similar to alarm clocks we use today. They prompt, remind or wake us up, to do something in particular.

Think about it for a moment. When you set your alarm, is it to wake you up for:

- Work?
- A meeting?
- A flight?
- School/College/University?
- Appointments?

Or is it a reminder to:

- Take your medication?
- Wish someone a happy birthday?
- Do something specific?

Whatever the reason, an alarm clock physically wakes us up by getting our attention. Once it has our attention it is there to serve as a reminder for us to '*do*' something. What that something is only you know, as that alarm is personally unique to you and your day. This is exactly the way 11:11 works, it is like one big alarm clock. It is trying to get our attention to wake us up to do something, to take action and change a situation.

This wake up call can be described as an awakening and is very similar to the film, The *Matrix*. *Neo* was led to Morpheus/Trinity who helped him wake up to reality.

Morpheus explains to Neo that the Matrix is an illusory world, created to prevent humans from discovering that they are slaves to an external influence. Holding out a capsule on each of his palms, he describes the choice facing Neo:

"This is your last chance. After this, there is no turning back. You take the blue pill — the story ends, you wake up in your bed and believe whatever you want to believe. You take the red pill — you stay in Wonderland, and I show you how deep the rabbit hole goes."

https://en.m.wikipedia.org/wiki/Red_pill_and_blue_pill

Just like Neo, without proper guidance a person who is going through an awakening such as 11:11 may be labelled with mental disorders or just plain old mad or crazy. When actually, they're just realising that most things around them are illusions. Here 11:11 acts like a glitch in the matrix of reality. It leaves us with two options to consider and choose:

1. *Blue pill* - that we're perpetually broken and that we're being infected with a virus that keeps filtering our reality in a very peculiar way.

2. *Red pill* - to consider that perhaps reality itself doesn't work the way we previously expected, and maybe, just maybe, these 11's are manifesting for a reason that we simply cannot comprehend at this moment in time.

Most people do their best to stick with the blue pill, choosing to ignore 11:11. They may cling to that pill for several months, years or perhaps their entire lives. But, many will eventually swallow the red pill and accept 11:11 has more to offer and will take that leap of faith and see where it leads. I took the red pill and I'd like to give you a glimpse into where it can lead:

My initial response to seeing 11:11 was to first ignore it. However, the more incessant it became the more curious I became. I would say; *"There must be more to this reality. What if there's some kind of intelligence behind it? What if something else is creating all these 11's to appear in my life, as a way of trying to get my attention?"*

The more questions I would ask, the more curious I would become. It was curiosity that led me down different avenues, whereby I found people and information to help me answer those questions.

The continued recurrence of 11:11 served as a constant wake-up call. I have to admit it can make it difficult to keep doing business as usual! Every time I thought I had life figured out, the 11:11 surge came back again, to remind me that there was more!

Eventually I concluded that my current understanding of reality must in fact be broken. That is when I began to embrace this 11:11 experience by stepping out of my comfort zone. Once I did this, it became clear that many of my assumptions about the nature of reality were wrong. Reality just didn't work the way I originally thought it did. I was stuck clinging to a broken model, but then I had something solid to replace it with 11:11. Think about it. What are you clinging to, the red pill or the blue pill?

Either way, do you feel awake and alerted by these numbers, but do not know what to do next? Maybe you still don't understand the meaning of 11:11 and nothing resonates with you? But, that's okay too because the meaning may arise once you are part way through your journey. Lessons with 11:11 are often learned midway through our experience. So do not worry if nothing is really sinking in yet, there is still a lot to cover.

***

Now that we have explored some of the key questions surrounding 11:11, Part 2 is about what to do now we see 11:11. But, to understand it you have to swallow that *'Red Pill'*, stepping away from all ideologies and the way you have been conditioned to think. It is being open minded and subject to change that is important.

So if you're ready to swallow that Red Pill, the next leg of this book are tools specifically designed, to help guide you through this process. I will be like your Morpheus, who guides you through your awakening. The aim is to explore, explain and describe ways into discovering what 11:11 wants and why it is in our lives. Trust me, there is a reason!

PART TWO

Tools for the Journey with 11:11 - What Do I Do Now? And How?

"To effectively communicate, we must realise that we are all different in the way we perceive the world and use this understanding as a guide to our communication with others."

Anthony Robbins

8

What Does 11:11 Want from Me?

Think about this for a moment:

- Have you ever been driving to pick a family member up from the train station and you honk your horn to get their attention?

- Whilst stood in a queue to pay for your shopping you see a friend. How do you get their attention? Do you jump up and down, frantically waving?

- When you're at a concert, do you jump up and down and point at yourself? Hoping that your idol will choose you to go on stage?

These are all ways that people try to get one's attention without speaking. This is exactly what the number 11:11 is like. It can't speak or shout at us to get our attention so, it jumps out at us in other ways. It is attempting to get our attention for a reason, it has a purpose. Do you want to find out what it wants? Maybe you will discover the deeper meaning or messages that are being conveyed to you, if you do.

Have you ever considered that 11:11's purpose in getting your attention, is to communicate something to you?

Communication is an important element in our everyday lives. Without it, we would not gain understanding or knowledge. The Oxford Dictionary defines communication as: *"The exchanging of information by speaking, writing or using some other medium"*. Think about it. What are all the different types of communication?

People communicate using different methods. Let's explore a few:

- Languages such as: English, French, German, Spanish, Hindi, Punjabi (are only a few).

- A blind person communicates using braille to read. They use talking devices to hear and guide dogs to direct and lead their way.

- A deaf person communicates using sign language, using body language, hands, fingers and gestures.

- Body language, gestures and expressions.

- Written Communication can come in forms of books, emails, letters, text messages and road signs to direct your way.

- Morse Code via sound alone.

So, why is 11:11 any different? Maybe it is communicating to people through the medium of numbers?

"So what do I do?" You may ask yourself. *"Do I just carry on ignoring it or do I communicate back?"*

Yes, as crazy as it may sound, what if you communicated to 11:11, just like you would with any other person? Maybe 11:11 just wants to chat? After all, the language is in the numbers, rather than the words.

9

What Do I Do When I See it?

Numbers are a universal language that everyone has the potential to understand. Plato called the study of numbers, *"the highest degree of knowledge."* If we seek knowledge-taking this statement into consideration, then surely we have something to gain, do we not? If 11:11 wants to communicate with us then shouldn't we reciprocate?

Think about it. If we can interpret, understand and learn the language that is being communicated to us, maybe we will find what we are so desperately seeking.

"So how do I communicate with 11:11?"

An easy way to help us to communicate with 11:11, is by using an acronym as a reminder. In this case the word would be **STAR**.

Every time you see 11:11, think *"STAR"*. Then run yourself through a simple procedure:

Stop
Think
Ask

Receive / Response

Let's first start by breaking each one of these headings down for you to understand.

Star Method - Step by Step Guide:

1. **Stop** to acknowledge the presence of this number.

2. **Think** about what you were doing at the very moment you saw 11:11. Turn your awareness goggles on. In other words, be alert and pay close attention to yourself and your surroundings:

What are you thinking? Maybe it is about work, a specific person, relationship or a problem? Maybe it is about a project or something that needs doing? Analysing your thoughts first when you see 11:11 can sometimes be helpful in deciphering the signs and messages being conveyed to you, through other senses described below.

What can you see? Can you see an advert, a road sign or a clip from a newspaper article? What does it say? Analyse everything you can see around you.

What can you hear? Can you hear a certain song playing on the radio in the background? Maybe, the lyrics are speaking to you? Did you overhear someone's words that 'clicks' with you? Maybe on the TV, radio, in conversation or in the background?

What can you smell? Can you smell a certain scent that reminds you of someone? Maybe a loved or deceased one?

What do you sense? Can you sense things, as if someone is whispering in your ear? Maybe you feel like someone is trying to tell you something? Do you feel like someone is nudging you in a certain direction or tapping you on the shoulder?

How do you feel? Do you feel angry, scared, sad, upset, confused? Maybe you feel positive, happy, peace, love, content? Perhaps you can look into the reasons why you are feeling like this.

Are any of these things resonating with you when you see it? Is a sign or something meaningful being conveyed to you, within the context of your life?

Pay attention, because these can be ways which 11:11 attempts to communicate with you. As an example:

I received a reminder letter from my doctors stating that I was due to have my cervical cancer screening and I needed to book an appointment. Obviously, I made up excuses in my head and put the letter to one side.

The next day I was in my car driving and I saw 11:11am on my clock. I immediately thought "STAR" and begun to run myself through this method. I stopped and thought about what I was thinking, nothing sprang to mind, I briefly glanced around and saw nothing of relevance but it was what I heard that pricked my ears. Yes, something caught my attention! On the radio was an advert about cervical screenings to prevent cancer. Hearing this gave me a flash back of my thoughts and feelings when getting that letter. For me 11:11 was a sign prompting me to make that appointment.

This is how 11:11 can work, it has the ability to prompt and remind us to do a specific thing. Guiding, reminding, alerting and perhaps even warning us towards something? Who knows, in this case preventing Cancer if found at an early stage?

Because this sign from 11:11 resonated with me I had no need to go through the whole method, this was enough. However, if nothing resonates then the next phase would be to 'ask'.

3. **Ask** 11:11 a question or for guidance.

You can ask a question by:

- Writing it down
- Speaking out loud
- Speaking in your head
- In your prayers

If you need guidance you can mentally say to yourself:

"If you are with me, please send me a sign."

"I am confused, please could you give me a direct sign."

"If I am on the right path can you show me a rainbow"

Then you must pay attention because when you least expect it, you will receive a sign. Sometimes we just need to stop, listen and interpret in order to understand or decode these signs. As an example:

When I was almost at the end of writing this book I was unsure if it was complete, I sat in bed and glanced at my iPad screen and 11:11pm caught my eye. Again, I ran myself through the STAR method, stopping for a moment to observe my surroundings. This time I zoned in on my thoughts, about whether my book was ready. In this instance, I called upon my Spirit 11:11 Guides (for me this was my Step Mum who had passed away) and I asked her for guidance by praying. I said "I really need your help. I need a sign, but I need a big sign from you this time. If this book is ready please guide me by presenting feathers to me." I sent out my request and fell asleep.

The next morning I was getting ready to take my son to nursery. As I walked out the front door my jaw dropped in shock at what I saw. On the floor were over a hundred feathers scattered on my driveway. I was shaking in disbelief and amazement! This was one of the biggest signs I received from my 11:11 guides. For me this was 100 percent confirmation that I was on the right track and my book was ready. For the first time (after numerous drafts) I finally felt content, reassured and happy that it was ready.

This is a prime example of how 11:11 responds to questions asked. 11:11 can help with anything, no job is too big or too small. This method also has another system you can try, even when you don't see 11:11 (this will be explored in Chapter 12).

Our 11:11 Spirit Guides can assist us with every area of our lives. They can help to heal ourselves, loved ones, or just to feel comforted and reassured. All we have to do is ask. As the old saying goes, *"If you don't ask, you won't receive".*

In my case I asked for feathers to be presented to me and I would like to share with you a poem entitled, 'Perfect Timing' which sums up feathers as signs:-

"I found a little sign today, just laying on the ground.
The feather that you sent me, when you knew I'd be around.
I know you're always helping, sending guidance from up
above and giving reassurance that I'm surrounded by your
love.
So I really want to Thank you for confirming that you're
there, at just the time I needed that little extra bit of care!"
Mary Jac

4. **Receiving** a response either instantly, within a few minutes, hours or days.

The above two examples used are only a few ways in which 11:11 can respond. In this experience it was instant, but please remember this took time for me to master. When you first try it you may not pick up on anything, it takes time and understanding and above all patience.

There are also many other ways 11:11 can respond, let's explore these in the next chapter in more detail.

10

How Can 11:11 Respond to Me?

Okay, so we know 11:11 can't directly, verbally communicate face to face with us. But it can communicate in other ways, these can be through signs, gentle nudges, gut feelings, intuitions or in our dreams. Let's explore these further:

Signs

Signs are pretty much everywhere we look. For example, when I am driving my car I see road signs everywhere. Can you imagine a world without road signs? Think about it. No traffic lights, no directions, no warning signs, no road markings, no speed limit signs! That would be one great big mess wouldn't it? These signs serve a purpose in preventing accidents and even death. They also comfort and reassure us when we are lost, making us feel safe and happy that we are headed in the right direction.

Well this is exactly how 11:11 works. Yes, 11:11 directs, guides, comforts and reassures us. It helps us to stay on the right track, just like road signs. When we see such signs be they road signs or signs from our 11:11 Spirit Guides, they visually stimulate our senses, sending messages to our brains to alert us to something. Signs points us towards something larger, bringing events that affect us to our attention.

We may not notice these signs the first time. But, if we run into the same or similar sign a second time, third time or in the case of 11:11 all the time, it would be wise to pay careful attention to it.

Sometimes our 11:11 Spirit Guides, will respond through signs and clues in our environment. They are like sign posts guiding us in the right direction or affirming our thoughts. These signs can come to us in the form of leaflets, posters, advertisements, license plates or a phone call from someone we haven't spoken to in a long time.

If we miss these signs, we may start to go off track. But rest assured, 11:11 will incisively begin to get our attention again. This can be a reason why seeing it can be so intense and frequent.

The signs are there if we know how and where to look and if the signs come looking for us, then it is worth taking notice just in case. The world is full of signs.

Whilst some messages are hidden, others are right in front of our eyes.

Gentle Nudges

Have you ever been going about your own business and suddenly, you feel the urge to get in touch with a certain person that you haven't talked to in a while or do something specific?

Our Spirit Guides can nudge us towards taking the necessary actions in order to meet the right people and take advantage of opportunities. It may feel like someone is whispering ideas or thoughts in your head. When this happens maybe we need to act upon those feelings?

Sometimes a nudge will seemingly come out of nowhere. Nudges tend to be time delayed. In other words, we ask a question from our Spirit Guides today, but they might not respond until a few hours, days or even weeks from now. But, if we keep our eyes wide open and pay attention we will receive them. This doesn't mean you go looking for them, they will come looking for you!

When they do respond though, it's usually an opportunity worth following up. Don't forget, it is essential to trust your intuition.

Intuition

Do you pay more attention to the patterns and possibilities that arise from your intuition? For example, the telephone rings and you intuitively know who it is before answering. Intuition often shows up this way, as a fleeting insight. Sometimes we may just write it off as a coincidence. However, *"is there such thing as a coincidence?"* Is it not synchronicity, teaching us to trust our inner selves?

For example, *I saw a missed call from my friend at 11:11am. A sudden urge overcame me, as if something was wrong. I couldn't pin point the reason why I felt like this, in fact there was no logical explanation for such feelings. I just had a feeling! So I called her back and she burst into tears. I asked her what was wrong and she told me her Dad had passed away.*

By trusting my intuition and following up on that instinct, I was able to support a friend in her time of need.

If we learn to trust our instincts our senses begin to open up. We rely on ourselves and our Spirt Guides, to communicate what we need to know. Our intuition can be seen as a connection to a Greater Intelligence.

When synchronicity and serendipity occurs, we should trust our instincts. The secret to hearing our intuition is learning to remain calm in all situations. This will open doors that we never imagined would be open to us.

Being patient is a virtue though. We should try to go with our gut feelings and intuitions, it is like an inbuilt Gps/Satnav that lays internally within us. It can direct us to our destination, if we just listen to it.

11:11 plays a significant role in our journey, if we allow it into our lives. Try not to underestimate it. It's like a tidal wave, go with the flow and see where it takes you.

Dreams

Do you ever experience dreams that are so vivid, you almost feel like you are awake? Many people refer to this as lucid dreaming or astral projection, whereby we are wakening to other areas outside of our bodies.

Maybe you see 11:11 in your dreams? If so could this be activating the awakening process, reminding us to seek knowledge surrounding 11:11 when awake? After all, when we dream we often wake up bewildered, confused and curious. Could these things set us on a quest to search for the meaning? When searching, perhaps we will be led to other signs and messages.

Dreams can offer clear, vivid and direct communication from our Spirit Guides. They can be metaphors or they can be literal, with the ability to show us likely future outcomes of different paths we might choose.

To get the most out of the messages we receive during dreams, we should keep a journal beside our bed, writing down important details of our dreams as soon as we wake up. This is a good tool to look back on, especially when it's fresh in our minds. We can also do this on a memo on our phone or download dream apps to help us with this.

"When you really pay attention, everything is your teacher."
Ezra Bayda

Remember that in some instances 11:11 can respond through one or several means, but we have to pay attention to *'what'* and *'how'* they are communicating to us.

11

Can 11:11 be a Response from a Loved One who has Passed Away?

Now let me give you an example through my personal experience of how Spirit Guides can communicate and respond to us via 11:11, by bringing together everything we have touched upon so far. This experience also highlights a common question asked about how 11:11 can represent and potentially be, a loved one who has passed away, responding to us.

I was in the car driving from London to Manchester to see my family. I was thinking about my Step Mum who had recently passed away. I was missing her a lot, wondering if she was okay wherever she was. All of a sudden a thought popped in my head. It was if someone was whispering in my ear, "Go and see a clairvoyant."

I then glanced at the clock and it was reading 11:11pm. On automatic pilot I thought of the STAR method. At that instance I noticed a song on the radio, it was Whitney Houston - "I Will Always Love You". This was one of my Step Mums favourite songs.

When I went to her house we would sit in the kitchen, have a drink and sing this song. This song was one of our favourites and had a lot of sentimental memories. I started to cry when I heard it and a sudden sense of relief and peace overcame my body. It felt as though she was with me. It had a personal meaning and message, which I felt was being communicated through this moment. For me this was a sign!

For the rest of the journey, all I could think about was my thoughts at the moment I saw 11:11.

(Recap - I was thinking about my Step Mum, wondering if she was okay. I then felt like I wanted to see a clairvoyant, and then our song came on. It was if my Angels were nudging me to act upon my thoughts. After these synchronistic moments, I was set on seeing someone and thought that when I got to Manchester I would ask my Sister in Law if she wanted to go with me).

The very next day I was playing with my baby and picked him up to walk into the kitchen. My Sister in Law was in there talking to her brother about how she went to see a clairvoyant and was in mid conversation talking about her experience. I was stunned, to say the least.

I told her what had happened on my journey up and how I was going to ask if she wanted to go with me (unaware she had already been). This was a moment of pure serendipity, I decided to trust my intuition and follow my Angels' (11:11) guidance.

I asked my Sister in Law for the clairvoyant's number so that I could call her to see if she would be able to see me. My Sister in Law said, "Yes, but I doubt you will get an appointment as I had to book mine three weeks in advance, but you can try".

I called the clairvoyant, hoping she would be available. "Yes, I have an appointment free for tomorrow. I don't normally work weekends but my husband is away on business so I am free." She said. (Talk about synchronicity!)

The next day I went to see her. I had three questions in my mind. The person I wanted to be present was my Step Mum. Before I went to see the clairvoyant, I did something a little bizarre and I don't know why I did it. However, I trusted my gut feeling and this is what I did:

I wrote three questions down that I needed answering and guidance with, which I wanted to ask my Step Mum. I then sent three emails with a question on each one. I sent them to myself, but in my head I was sending them to my Step Mum. With my three separate emails sent, an hour later I had my appointment with the clairvoyant.

I didn't really know what I was expecting as I had never visited a clairvoyant before. However, I remained open minded and decided to give nothing away, except 'Yes' or 'No' answers. I suppose that was my way of testing if she was a phoney or not.

What happened in the reading was amazing! My Step Mum came to me and made herself known straight away. She knew everything about me. She communicated through the clairvoyant telling me that she was with me on a daily basis. She communicated how she listens to me and guides me when I ask for advice or support. This was true as I spoke to her in my head almost everyday.

She continued to talk about other things such as relationship advice to what I had been doing with my baby. This confirmed to me that the spirit realm was very much real. But nothing could have prepared me for what happened next!

My Step Mum said, "I've got the notes you sent me. I have them here on three separate pieces of paper. The answer to those questions are in your dreams."

I instantly knew what she meant by this, although the clairvoyant was looking rather confused. She kept asking me, "Does this make sense?" And I would nod in agreement, still not wanting to give anything away until the end of the reading.

All the questions I thought about everyday. They were problems that I faced and for me, the only way those problems could be solved was by moving to another house. Everyday, I dreamt about my new home. What it would look like and how all my problems would disappear. I would dream so much that it would motivate me to work harder, to save the money to get there. Once I had the money, all my problems would fade away. That was what my Step Mum meant, by "The answer is in your dreams."

I felt relieved but I was shaking uncontrollably, shocked that this clairvoyant was not a phoney. There was no possibility that she could have known that I sent three separate emails with questions to my Step Mum.

By the end of the session I was so emotional, I couldn't stop crying. Still to this day, I have the three emails I sent and I also recorded the session. I listen to it on a regular basis as it gives me hope and strength when times get tough. For me, this was confirmation that she was okay. I felt reassured to know that she was safe and watching down on me.

As I left and walked out the door, a feather landed on my foot and I knew that my Angelic Step Mother was with me.

This is one example of how 11:11 works. 11:11 is like a radio station, we have to tune in to follow. Obviously in my case I saw 11:11 and I just so happened to tune into the radio station in the background. If I wasn't tuned in, I would never have heard that song and then followed up on it. It was this moment that led me towards the right direction of answering questions I needed. And, also receiving clear messages from my beloved Step Mum who had passed away. This in itself was comforting and reassuring.

I learned that I had to be open to doing new things and having new experiences. When we are open to 11:11 and perhaps other synchronistic events, they act as guidance, which can help us make choices in our lives.

"A mind is like a parachute. It doesn't work if it's not open." Frank Zappa.

As you can see the STAR method can be a foundation to begin understanding 11:11, if we follow up on it. It can also serve as a valuable tool, with the ability to help us focus on the number when we see it. It can further encourage us to harness our direct attention towards our surroundings, both internally and externally. This can take time to master but patience is a virtue.

Being aware of the signs 11:11 attempts to convey to us is important. Our commitment to trust what is shown to us is equally significant. When in doubt we can hand over or call upon our Spirit Guides, to help us move through each moment that we need help with.

If you wonder what the signs are that your 11:11 Spirit Guides show you, ask them to be clear if need be. If you feel 11:11 is a representation of a loved one who has passed away, ask them to give you a sign. For example, I have spoken to many people who have lost someone they love. They feel that they communicate through 11:11. Sometimes they see 11:11 and someone walks past them wearing the same cologne/aftershave that their Loved one wore. Or, someone says something to them that their loved one used to say.

These are all prime examples of 11:11 guiding us with the support of someone we loved and lost. However, remember that they act as guides. They still leave us to figure many things out for ourselves. Now let me show you ways to work these things out within the next chapter!

12

How Do I Build up My Vocabulary Using it?

Once we have a level of understanding of the STAR method, we can then progress to communicating with 11:11 in other ways. It is like building up our vocabulary to this new found language, but in the form of other signs and symbols. Remember it's not all about seeing 11:11. Now we are awake, perhaps 11:11 is taking us deeper down that rabbit hole!

An easy way to help us build up our own, unique vocabulary with 11:11, is by using another acronym as a reminder. In this case the word would be **GATEWAY.** You can try this method even when you don't see 11:11. This can be a particularly good tool to use if you are struggling to grasp the STAR method or believe that 11:11 could be a Divine Force.

Run yourself through this simple procedure:

Give Gratitude

Ask

Think

Envision

Wait

Anticipate

You will receive

GATEWAY Method – Step by Step Guide

1. **Give Gratitude** to 11:11 for being present in your life.
2. **Ask** your Spirit Guides for guidance by calling them to you. Once you have called them be specific about the kind of support you want. As an example:

"11:11 Spirit Guides, I call upon you to help me on the project I am working on. If I am heading in the right direction please confirm this to me." Then..

3. **Think** about an item.

It can be anything, from rainbows, ladybirds, stars to phoenixes, bears or bananas. These are just a few examples, choose something that holds meaning to you. Really visualise this item. Once you have chosen that item (as an example I chose a phoenix), then...

4. **Envision** a beam of light encapsulating your very being and visualise your Spirit Guides. Call upon them to show you a sign, through the symbol you have chosen by saying,

"If I am on the right track please present to me phoenixes as a sign to confirm this."

5. **Wait** patiently for a sign and...

6. **Anticipate** a sign or message to be communicated to you.

7. **You will receive** a response, by that item being presented to you in some shape or form if you are on the right track.

Let me now illustrate this strategy with a personal experience:

I wanted to know if I was on the right track, so I called upon my 11:11 Spirit Guides asking for their guidance. I then envisioned and visualised a phoenix and then affirmed this image by asking my Guides to present this to me, if I was on the right track.

I let this go, having faith that they would respond. When using this GATEWAY method over the course of several days, I began seeing phoenixes everywhere.

First I was walking down the street and a business van drove passed and its brand name was "Phoenix foods". The same day I was given a leaflet from a Buddhist monk about events they had on and on the front of this leaflet was a picture of a Phoenix.

Then I was really blown away when I was unpacking a box to look for my photo album and I came across a book my Mother had published over 18 years ago. I didn't know this (but I do now) the picture on the front of her cover was a picture of a Phoenix! For me all the synchronised events that unfolded were divinely orchestrated to convey a message to me, that I had asked through such signs. This for me was further confirmation that I was on the right track.

The funny thing is after I wrote this extract, a few hours later, I turned on a children's tv programme for my son to watch. And you will never guess what happened. The character held up a sign and the words written on it was "Phoenix". Now that is what I call synchronicity at its finest! This example was meant to be in this book and it was affirmed through such happenings.

This was the fun of the 11:11 signs and messages. It was taking me on a journey from numbers to seeing other signs and symbols such as phoenixes. All I had to do was ask a direct question, that I would understand. Not only this, but it also serves as a great reminder many years later.

"Ask for what you want and be prepared to get it."
Maya Angelou

These were interpreted and found by playing around with 11:11, by utilising the GATEWAY method. Remember we can have fun with our new found 11:11 friend too. Try not to take the friendship too seriously! Why not try it for yourselves? Build up your own dictionary of meanings by asking for guidance, reassurance, warnings, the list is endless.

When building up your vocabulary though, it is also important not to fear this experience and to be open minded. The signs that we get are to remind, comfort or reassure us that our Spirit Guides are with us at all times. It can also act as confirmation if we are struggling to believe and need proof with physical eyes. This gives us confirmation through signs, that they are answering questions that we may pose.

By embracing this extraordinary experience, we activate the power of these numbers. If we try unplugging our fears, we may come to terms with this experience and feel more at ease. Remember to have faith in 11:11 because it will give you a solid foundation when embarking on your journey.

13

What are The Foundations to 11:11?

Bringing Part Two to a close, 11:11 can be viewed as, a wakeup call that is frantically trying to get our attention. Once we accept that it is attempting to grab our attention for a reason, we then need to start paying attention. The key is not to look too much into how we keep seeing 11:11, but what it is trying to communicate to us. It is only then we will truly understand what it means.

This may not happen straight away. It takes time, practice, patience and perseverance, but that is part of the journey. For me personally it has taken several years for me to understand what 11:11 means and what it wants. But, once we step outside our comfort zone and start communicating with 11:11 the more open we become. It is then that we learn to understand the significance of 11:11 in our lives. Let me illustrate this with a scenario:

Try to imagine 11:11 as a person you met at a bus stop. You don't know that person, in fact they're a complete stranger to you. But then all of a sudden they grab your attention by smiling at you. Think about it. What do you do? Do you smile back and say hello or do you ignore them? The choice is ultimately yours.

If you smile back, you are connecting with them through non-verbal communication. By smiling back, they then start to talk to you. *"How is your day?"* This could lead to a number of scenarios. Maybe, you will find out something interesting about this person? Perhaps you knew them or have previously crossed paths with them? What if you end up exchanging telephone numbers and go out? Who knows, even resulting in marriage or babies?

The point is you would never know unless you made that move. You would never know unless you communicated to them. This is how 11:11 works, you have to make that move and communicate with it.

Experiencing 11:11 is like having a relationship, you have to build trust and have faith in where it will take you. Trust and faith are the foundations of building up your relationship with 11:11. *"But how do I build this relationship?"* You may ask.

If we treat 11:11 as if it is our friend we have a lot to gain in many different ways. Think about a good friend you have and what makes them a good friend? If we use 11:11 with the thought that it is our friend and apply these attributes that make a 'good friend' it will, guide, reassure and comfort us. It will also respond to our questions if only we ask. Faith and trust in our 11:11 friend can clear space for Divine support.

As we begin to open up to what 11:11 has to offer, we become much more aware and sensitive to our surroundings. This is when synchronicity showers our lives with blessings and abundance. The journey that once began with the number synchronicity, such as 11:11 will then lead us onto other paths. These paths then lead us to other signs, symbols and numbers. Thus leading us one step closer to our destination.

Sometimes life can be tough but if we try to have faith in the number 11:11 when we see it and consider faith to be the bedrock of what we do, then when we stumble upon difficulty and our vision is clouded, faith can give us hope and strength.

Communicating with faith gives us the greatest gift of all-Vision. I remember once asking my mother who was an author and also partially blind; *"Can there be anything worse than losing your sight?"*

"Yes, there can" she replied, *"losing your vision"*.

It is important not to lose sight of the visions and opportunities that 11:11 presents. Not only is faith important with 11:11 but so is trust. Trust is something that we must build into a relationship and then it needs to be valued and maintained. Our sense of security with 11:11 can be seen like any other relationship. When we learn to trust, we are free to be ourselves, without feeling any need to guard our heart.

When we feel safe and secure that 11:11 means no harm and is here as a guide, we grow. Grow to understand that it is here to help us. It is then that we no longer need to hide our true feelings or raise our defences. The walls come down and love expands. When love expands, we are then guided by our heart.

The key to our treasures lies within our own possession. We have the choice to either keep the key hidden away, collecting dust, sitting there doing nothing with no true purpose. Or the other option is to use the key, by picking it up and taking a chance to walk through those doors of opportunities, which 11:11 presents to us. If we choose to take action and walk through these doors into the unknown, who knows where it may lead us? But do you take that chance? Well, that is your choice!

PART THREE

The Never Ending Journey - Can 11:11 Change My Life?

"The secret of change is to focus all of your energy, not on fighting the old, but on building the new." Socrates

I Keep Seeing 11:11 Do You?

14

Why Have I Not Seen 11:11 for a While?

11:11's presence at first can feel like it is stalking us, but once we begin to accept it's presence means no harm we begin to relax. We grow accustomed to this presence popping out of nowhere and sometimes catching us off guard. But what does it mean when it abruptly stops and we don't see it for a while?

Do you ever go through spells of seeing 11:11 then nothing for a few weeks or months? Do you wonder what the reason could be, especially when 11:11 is normally so persistent in getting your attention.

Here are a few possibilities to consider:

Changes in your life: Many have ascribed experiencing seeing 11:11 more when they are going through significant changes in their lives.

Think about it. When you saw 11:11 previously, were you going through any changes? This could be relationship, family, work issues or even a loved one passing away? Once all these issues began to resolve, did you feel like you were going in the right direction?

Maybe that is when you stopped seeing it or it became less frequent?

Already Awake: 11:11 is a guide to support and nudge us when we need it the most. Maybe you already have the awareness that you need to move forward on your path. If you have that awareness maybe 11:11 does not need to make an appearance. It may even be that 11:11 has served it's purpose by waking you up.

Vision is clouded: If life throws obstacles your way, maybe the stresses of life are impeding your vision? When life is tough we sometimes do not pay attention to our surroundings because we are consumed by physical and emotional problems. Are you experiencing a variety of problems in your life? Do you feel emotionally drained or lost?

Maybe all you need to do is clear your mind. If we clear our minds then we may have vision to see 11:11. Could it be that these factors are making us less receptive in paying attention, that we are not noticing it anymore? If so, perhaps try meditation, affirmation and gratitude techniques to help declutter your mind. When the mind is clear we gain clarity and our vision is then restored.

Too focused on seeing 11:11: It could even be that you started to see 11:11 but other signs, symbols and even other number sequences are trying to get your attention now? Maybe we are too focused on 11:11 we are missing other signs and numbers around us. Try not to focus too much on it, tunnel vision can limit you. Remember 11:11 opens up other doors and avenues to guide us. It's not all about 11:11.

However, if it is really concerning you and you feel like you need it back in your life, just ask. We can bring it back into our lives simply by asking our Spirit Guides. This can be done by saying:

"I have not seen you (11:11) for a while. If you're still with me please show yourself."

If we need guidance, again ask, remembering the GATEWAY method. This principle can be used even when we don't see it.

Whatever the reason we've stopped seeing 11:11, try not to over think the reasons why. Remember, everything happens for a reason and who knows it may pop back into your life at some point.

15

What are Other People's Experiences, Thoughts and Beliefs Surrounding 11:11?

I have spent many years collecting information and conversing with people all over the world. This not only helped me on my journey, but it also gave me an insight into how the interpretation of 11:11 can vary person to person.

I would now like to share with you a small handful of personal interactions I have had with others on their personal insights and experiences with 11:11. Perhaps you may relate to some of them.

"I Keep seeing 11:11. My Dad passed away on 11/1/11 and I feel that when I see this number sequence that it is my Dad talking to me."
Jaycee - Big Spring, Texas

"I was born on 11th November (11/11) and it has followed me all my life. I've been investigating numerology and many other spiritual & self-aware things for at least 7 years. I have

learned to follow the signs. I also know that my Angels are guiding me, too."

Maria - Argentina.

"I've been seeing 11:11 for a year. Since then it has been a life altering experience, in that my life has done a total flip! I am not the same person I was before experiencing it. Since then I have had many spiritual-related things occur. For me it was an awakening to my lightworker work - to realize that I need to start using my 3rd-eye and spiritual abilities to help other people."

Kim Szuta - Calgary Alberta, Canada

"I have been seeing 11:11 for about 5 years. At first I thought it was a coincidence, I even started to explain this to my friends and room mates. I can't explain how many times my eyes stop on this number. Yesterday I was talking on the phone and when I finished I saw that the call duration was 11:11. When I see it I have peace of mind."

Juthy - Bangladesh

"I know 11:11 to be a spiritual sign. I find it mysterious that so many others are having the same experience. Maybe it is a nudge to an awakening and God is telling those that see 1111

to pay attention- to re unite, collectively changing the consciousness of this world one person at a time."
Greg Doniger - Dallas, Texas

"I started seeing those numbers on November 11th 2013. Since then, my life changed a lot. I started solving my karma among my past relationships by giving a good closure to it. After that, I realised that I was only surviving to get a low salary teaching classes for over 12 years. I then decided to become an artist, a love and passion I have. Although money was not important to me in the past, I now respect myself and my self-worth, so in this new career change, money and energy started to flow back again. I don´t talk much about the 11:11 thing to my friends, because they think thats weird, although I have tried before."
Andrea Jen - Argentina

"For the past month I see 1111 so many times a day. I remember it first started after I began reading a book on how to raise your vibrations. After I had read it I fell asleep and had a dream about 11:11. Usually I NEVER remember my dreams, but in this dream I remember standing in front of a store and my whole attention turned to the stores number 1111. Then I immediately woke up and automatically thought, 'Spirit Guides' and I was super excited. Then the

next day I read another book and it was talking about numerology. So synchronicity here??? Well ever since that night, I see 1111 everywhere. I looked it up with numerology and I thought to myself like, 'oh I must be on the right path'. So now every time I see 1111 know I am on the right track and I give gratitude to my Spirit Guides."
Kammilah- California

"11:11 are my Spirits and Angels letting me know that my spiritual awakening is ascending. Whenever I see 11:11 I become aware of my thoughts and surroundings."
Lexus - Texas

"Physical reality is a consciousness created by digital codes. Numbers define our existence. Human DNA, our genetic memory, is encoded to be triggered by digital codes at specific times and frequencies. These codes awaken the mind to the change and evolution of consciousness. I feel that 11:11 is one of those codes when I see it, it basically means that I am on the right path. I also smile when I see it."
Eric Youngren - NYC

"What I love most about 11:11 is that it is an "experience" that people cannot deny is happening to them. At first they'll try to rationalize it, but logic can't prevail in this case. After

a while they realize it's happening to others as well, which is sometimes a relief, but actually creates more questions than it answers. And that's the point... Because if this is happening, the world is not how we may have believed it was. There's something more going on!!

I also love that in a simple way 11:11 unites us. People all across the world of all ages "see" it. I believe it provides us with a reminder to come together and connect with each other and spirit when we see the numbers. Our Unity is so powerful.

But 11:11 also plays another role. Since numbers carry vibration, the resonance of this master number sequence is actually waking up our DNA and helping us to evolve our consciousness. Sometimes we are so focused on the "meaning" that we forget there's another function for the numbers. 11:11 is an Awakening Code".

Julie Ann - Singapore

These are all extracts of other people's insights, experiences and interpretations of what 11:11 means to them. As you can see they're all different interpretations. There is no right or wrong, the meaning is what resonates within each individuals heart.

11:11 takes everyone on a different journey, where some people's perceptions of it may change with time. I hope that after reading this book, your perception may feel somewhat clearer. I would like to also take this opportunity to express my gratitude to all these kind souls for sharing a piece of their 11:11 journey and puzzle with the world.

16

Can Your Perception of 11:11 Change?

With deeper understanding and working in line with 11:11, thoughts and feelings may change. When many people awaken and step outside of their comfort zone with curiosity their perception begins to alter.

When we are curious, we see things differently. We use our powers of observation more fully. We sense what is happening in the present moment, taking note of what is, regardless of what it looked like before or what we might have expected it to be. It is the curiosity in our souls that looks and asks questions, which take us to our destination. So *Ask, ask, ask!* This is when and where the magic happens. It is only then, that we are able to interpret the meaning behind 11:11 in much more depth.

We are also able to take the first movements into stepping outside our comfort zones and seeking the meanings to life and it's messages. Not many people are comfortable at first with the idea that Spirit Guides are giving us direction. The key to accessing synchronicity is to be receptive (remember, be the magnet). In this instance, synchronicity arrives in the form of number sequences.

Now it is part of our lives, we should not fear it, but love it. After all, we are all born with love, fear is just what we learn. The journey is about unlearning our fears and bringing love back into our hearts. Therefore, we should embrace this moment with love and accept it as a gift. It is a powerful, spiritual and positive number that illuminates the path we walk on. It is on our side!

"The important thing is not to stop questioning. Curiosity has its own reason for existing." Albert Einstein.

After exploring the 11:11 phenomenon and putting these tools to use you may begin to feel different. Obviously, you have to put these things into action to see a result first. But once you do, perhaps your perception will change.

Now think about this... Do you remember how it used to make you feel when you saw 11:11 everywhere for the first time? I do (go back to the introduction for a recap if needed).

For me when I see 11:11 now it:

- Makes me jump up and down in excitement
- Makes my heart race faster with love

- Makes me laugh and smile with joy

It used to affect me physically but also mentally. But now I understand what 11:11 means I now feel:

- Happy
- Loved
- Comforted
- Reassured
- Guided
- On the right track

My thought process changed to:

- "This is not a coincidence, this is synchronicity."
- "It is not chance, I see it for a reason."
- "There it is again! Thank you 11:11 for being part of my journey."
- "I can't wait to see you again."
- "This is the most amazing feeling in the world."
- "Thank you for communicating with me."
- "11:11 is my wake up call."
- "I am not alone."

In the course of my journey my feelings about 11:11 significantly changed. The way that I see it now is much different to the beginning of my journey. That is because with time and through experience alone I learned what 11:11 meant to me, by connecting those dots to see the bigger picture. You too have the opportunity to find out, by using the tools I have shared. The knowledge from this book is 11:11's gift to you, communicated through me!

17

Shall I Summarise 11:11 for You?

Yes, let's summarise everything off in One chapter now!

The experience of seeing the prompt 11:11 leads you on your own unique journey. Sometimes it can be difficult to describe what seeing 11:11 means, because it is a personal experience for everyone. If you feel you are having these experiences for a reason, then it might be that only you will know what these number prompts and wake up calls could mean.

The first step though, is acknowledging the presence of 11:11 in your life. At the beginning of your journey you may not know what 11:11 is or what it means. Questions arise in your mind, such as:

"I don't know what it means?"
"I don't have a clue why I keep seeing them?"
"I've been seeing them for years and still don't know the meaning?"

But, how can those questions be answered if you don't actively search? It's like cooking a cake. Think about it.

If you don't know how to make a chocolate cake and you really wanted to know the recipe, what would you do?

Well, if I really wanted to know something I would do something about it. I would get up and find out. I would ask. I would read. I would search until I found that recipe. I would most likely come across hundreds of different chocolate recipes, but I would choose the one that catches my eye and that I feel I would like. Then I would make that cake and sit down and enjoy the pleasure of eating it. That is what I would do! What would you do? Would you do anything different? Or would you just sit there and wonder?

You're probably thinking, "*What does a chocolate cake recipe have to do with seeing the number 11:11?*" The question is, "*What is the difference from finding that chocolate cake recipe, to finding out why I keep seeing the number 11:11?*" This was the question I asked myself so many times on so many different occasions.

The answer: Acting upon your intentions by searching, listening, asking and paying attention to yourself and your surroundings. You have to be actively involved in it all. Remember that communication is a two-way process, we are not bystanders but active participants!

Actions are what grabs someone's attention. It is the driving force behind everything. It teaches, it leads, it sets examples, but above all it is our actions that create change. Many people say *"I want something"*. But wanting is nothing more than a mere dream and desire. It is the actions that turn those dreams into reality.

For example I needed to change my mindset about 11:11. This is how I did it (maybe if you changed your mindset you could do it too?)

1. Change, **"I want to know about 11:11"** into, **"I will find out about 11:11"** You will then have a starting point.

2. Then turn it into an intention, **"I am going** to do a Google search on 11:11."

3. Then physically act upon your intention, **"I have just googled 11:11 on the internet."**

Now you are actively doing something and putting your purpose, feelings, thoughts into practice.

4. Once you have done it, **"I have found out possible explanations into what 11:11 could mean."**

Thus the aim, purpose and goal has been achieved. You are able to turn your questions into answers and gaining something by doing four simple things:

1. Knowing
2. Intending
3. Doing
4. Achieving.

Knowing and intending are the thoughts in our minds. However, it is the doing that gets us to our destination. It is the doing, that achieves our goals and what we are seeking. It is the actions of actively doing something, that make those questions form into reality. Let me illustrate this example with a personal experience with 11:11's guidance.

I was staying at My Nan's house for the weekend and I was telling her how I wanted to write a book. She would look at me like I had lost the plot, shake her head and say, "You are such a dreamer, I don't believe what you say, I believe what you do." Powerful words which really made me think.

I sat in bed that night, with my Nan's words cutting deep within me. "How could anyone take me seriously?" I thought.

Whilst I was thinking, I glanced at the time '11:11 pm'. Yes, there it was again. As soon as I saw it I put the STAR method into action. This time, I paid attention and analysed my thoughts. I was thinking about my book and this was a sign for me to follow up on my dreams and put it into action. After all, when I see 11:11 my thoughts have the ability to manifest.

That night I decided I had to change. I needed to start doing what I was saying because my words were meaningless and I wanted to be heard and seen. I remember saying to myself, "I will show my Nan!"

I realised that all I ever did was say things, I never actually did them and my Nan realised this about me. She was right though, I was a dreamer. But now I wanted my dreams to become a reality.

I realised that if I really wanted something, I had to get off my backside, work hard using willpower and patience to succeed. I had to "Just Do It!" That is when I started to put my words into actions and I began writing.

Over a period of several months I worked hard in achieving my goals. I won't lie, sometimes I had moments where I felt as though I couldn't write anymore because I lost focus and drive. Then for a few weeks I would stop writing. That is when I started to see 11:11 repeatedly. It was through this sighting that I was reminded to stop for a moment and think about where I was. I would ask for guidance. I would call 11:11 my, "Mr Motivator" as when I saw it, it kept me focused towards my new found project, which I was about to embark on.

Two years later, I achieved my goal because you are now reading it!

This is the power of 11:11. If we align our thoughts and pay attention to our surroundings, we are guided in the right direction to help us manifest our deepest desires.

To change your way of thinking-try to change: "I can't understand 11:11" into, "I can understand 11:11"

"It is impossible to find the meaning of 11:11" into, "it is possible to find the meaning of 11:11!"

"There is no way to understand 11:11" into, "There is always a way!"

"Other people will think it's crazy" into, "Who cares, it's my life, I am not crazy I am an 11:11 limited edition!"

All we have to do is change our thoughts to CHANGE our life. We will then be one step closer to achieving our goals or finding out the meaning, so that we can move forward.

Through changing our thoughts, the world is our oyster. Take that chance on 11:11 by applying four simple principles, called the 4 C's:

1. Choices
2. Chances
3. Create
4. Change

If we don't make a choice, to take a chance on 11:11 then will our lives ever move or change? Think about it. When you look back into your past, was everything in your life a reflection of the choices that you made and the chances that you took?

These are two by-products which play a pivotal role in changing our lives for the better. If we want a different result, then we have to make different choices. Our choice to change depends upon the way we think. Things begin to change when we act, rather than just question and dream. Perhaps 11:11 is just prompting us to remind us to do that specific something.

The journey that began with 11:11 has the ability to take us on a journey to other things, which can help us on the road to where we are going. Trust in 11:11 it too acts. Acts to guide, help, support, reassure, comfort and to direct us. All we have to do is have faith, step out of our comfort zones and jump. If we don't use that action of jumping, we won't get anywhere. So perhaps we should act now and take that leap of faith into the unknown.

Remember, the experience of seeing 11:11 is personally unique to us all. For some it is just a nuisance. For others it is a wake up call. It may even be our Spirit Guides, just wanting to communicate something to us? Perhaps it takes us a little further into discovering who we are or what our purpose is? But, if we don't actively act to find out what it means, we will never find out the meaning behind it. So act now, in order to discover, learn and grow with this beautiful experience. And always remember, you are not alone!

18

How Do I Find Like Minded People?

There is nothing worse than feeling alone is there? That is how the 11:11 experience can make people feel. At times it may feel like it's only happening to you. Especially when you are going through an experience that friends or family members don't understand. They may look at you like you've lost the plot, when you try to explain what has been going on with these number sequences.

It may get to a point where you give up talking about it, in fear that others think you are *'strange'* or *'crazy'*. Possibly you will retreat back within yourself, which can make you feel isolated. I know these feelings all too well!

One of the very first things I came to realise when I first began to experience the 11:11 phenomenon was how difficult it was to discuss this with other people. They found it extremely difficult, to wrap their brains around this concept. This being due to the fact that they didn't understand it or were not experiencing it. Clearly, this is understandable.

However, now you know that you are not alone in this experience and that millions of other people are experiencing this, perhaps you could connect with them? *"But, how?"* You may ask yourselves.

There are many groups and networks on the internet that I personally have found helpful, where you can discuss and share your experiences, get more information and ask questions from people who are also sailing in the ocean of one, one, one, one!

I would now like to invite you into that sea of Ones by giving you resources to stumble across at your leisure and desire. These are a combination of Twitter, Facebook, Websites and email sources from dear friends and 11:11 associates.

They have all kindly agreed and given their permission to share their social details so that they can help you on the course of your journey with 11:11. Perhaps it will lead you down a road of discovery and further your insight by connecting with others who are experiencing this 11:11 phenomenon.

The 11:11 Team

Natasha Nanda

Feel free to connect with me:

Twitter: 11:11 @Ikeepseeing1111
https://mobile.twitter.com/ikeepseeing1111

Facebook: I Keep Seeing 11:11- Community
https://www.facebook.com/pages/I-keep-seeing-1111/391104494378478?ref=ts&fref=ts

Website: **www.Ikeepseeing1111.com**

Email: **ikeepseeing1111@gmail.com**

Julie Anne- Founder of Global Vision 11:11

Do you see 11:11 or 222, 333, 555? Whenever you see 11:11, use the reminder to send out your vision for the world and connect with others in a global wave of joy. Don't see 11:11? Join anyway, it's all about unity! A daily wave of positive intention. For more in depth information on 11:11, visit the website.

Twitter: Global Vision 11:11 @keepseeing1111
https://mobile.twitter.com/KeepSeeing1111

Facebook: Global Vision-11:11- Community
https://www.facebook.com/seeing1111

Website: **www.seeing1111.com**

Steve- Founder of Wave 11:11

Wave 11:11 is about unity, awareness and awakening to who you truly are and who you are not, while setting intentions on unconditional love as the focal point.

We are all in a journey of remembrance whose purpose is to connect us to the essences of our souls and the understanding that all is One. We are here to awaken from our illusion of separateness. 11:11 is One Collective Consciousness: Joy, Love Peace and Unity.

Twitter: Wave 11:11 @Wave1111
https://mobile.twitter.com/Wave1111

Facebook: Wave1111- Community
https://www.facebook.com/theWave1111

Website: **www.wave1111.com**

Solara- Author

The 11:11 Doorway is the bridge between duality and Oneness. *"11:11 - Inside the Doorway"* is a book written and published in 1992. A more recent book is, *"The Star-Borne: A Remembrance for the Awakened Ones"* which contains information on 11:11.

My focus and mission is on our massive transformational journey through the 11:11 Doorway. The 11:11 Doorway is enabling us to shift from a duality-based reality to the Ultra Greater Reality.

Within the 11:11 Doorway, there are Eleven Gates, or frequency bands of energy. Each Gate that is activated births new levels of awareness that have not been on this planet before. More information on the 11:11 Doorway is available on the website.

Facebook: 11:11 Doorway- Community
https://www.facebook.com/1111Doorway

Websites:
www.nvisible.com
www.journey.emanaku.com
www.anvisible.com

Cassidy Cayne- Founder of Twin Flames 11:11
My Twin Flame and I have a personal mission to help as many people as possible reunite with their Twin Flame in love. When Twin Flames come together we also contribute to elevating consciousness on the planet.

I have been asked by spirit to share my experience in the form of a clear, concise course to help other Twins through the Ascension process with ease and grace.

When I started my journey, I had no one to turn to for help, so I decided to start a community for Twin Flames on my blog which can be found on my website, where we can share our experiences and give each other advice and support.

Twitter: Twin Flames 11:11 @twinflames_1111
https://mobile.twitter.com/TwinFlames_1111

Facebook: Twin Flames 11:11-Website
https://www.facebook.com/twinflames1111

Website: **www.twinflames1111.com**

Sarah Cherry- Founder of Angels 11:11
Did you wake up last night, check the time and see 11.11 or 4.44? Do you notice repeating number sequences on receipts or in phone numbers? Your Angels have a message for you. It's easy to interpret once you know the spiritual meaning of numbers. Feel free to connect for inspiring quotes, information and to share your own insights or ask questions.

Facebook: Angels 11:11- Community
https://www.facebook.com/Sarahs.Angels11.11

Georgina Beament- Founder of 11:11 Awakening

11:11 is calling you. Are you listening? Our mission is to answer our higher calling - which we know on some level is being triggered by 11:11 - and to ACT on the principles we know to be true and good: Love, kindness, peace, forgiveness, health, joy, gratitude, ascension, bliss.

From some of our posts, a few people wonder if we are a religion. To that we say yes! We are the Religion of Love, and in that religion we are all minsters.

Facebook: Awakening Code Community 11:11 22:22 33:33- Public Group.

(This Public group is a beautiful site where people can connect and share their experiences and thoughts with others who see 11:11 and other number sequences. It is highly interactive and a good place to have discussions. Due to it being a public group you will have to search the above once connected to Facebook.)

11:11 Awakening- Education
https://www.facebook.com/pages/1111-Awakening-Code/141194563292

***

I hope these sources help you on your journey. Remember, you are not alone! Regardless of race, colour or creed, you can take part in the experience of 11:11. People from all over the globe are conversing, that alone shows the power of this phenomenon bringing people together.

It may sound small and insignificant, but a small spark can start a great fire. Perhaps the 11:11 discussion will inspire people to come together and focus on spiritual matters. As they do, they raise their spiritual vibrations, thus helping the whole of humanity.

This is not the end, this is just the beginning of your adventure. Start connecting with others, who knows where this road of meeting like-minded people will take you? Good luck and remember...

Do Not Fear 11:11
Embrace it.

Thank you for walking with me on my journey. For me this is not the end, it is only the beginning. I hope that I have played a part in helping you on your journey.

Natasha Nanda

ACKNOWLEDGEMENTS

I would like to finish with the credits of this book by, expressing my sincere gratitude to all those who have helped me on my journey. Without these people and significant others I would not have been able to complete this book. Thank you to...

11:11 - For giving me the biggest wake up call and grabbing my attention by popping out of the blue in the most wondrous and mind boggling ways. Thank you for your guidance, motivation, inspiration, reassurance and support. You lifted me up in ways that gave me strength, hope and belief. You helped me out in times of need and showed me the way.

Because of your presence in my life I have been blessed to meet other people who experience this phenomenon. Through this, it has opened up doorways for me to heal my own past problems and to give hope and light to others who have shared similar painful experiences as myself. You have been my light that has led me out of the darkness.

Thank you for being my muse, whispering, nudging and presenting signs to me, to complete my mission in helping others with this 11:11 phenomenon.

Sheila Bassi - my beautiful Step Mother, thank you for being there and supporting me when I first had the idea about my book. I remember all the chats on the phone we had. You were the only person who didn't think I was going crazy and if you did, you would have made a great actress!

In 2014 part way through writing my book, you passed away and left us here on this physical plane. You left a hole in my heart as the beautiful, bubbly, kind, caring and loving soul left me. But I know you are in a better place. It was never "goodbye", it is "I will see you later."

Thank you for guiding me from up above and being there when I needed it the most. Thank you for responding to my calls through signs and messages. I love you lots and I know that you will be looking down on me, proud that I have completed my book. This one is dedicated to you!

Nikhil Nanda - My Best friend, Lover, Husband and Soulmate. Thank you for listening to my craziness. I know you knew I was mad before I married you, but I don't think anything prepared you for when I told you I was writing a book on 11:11. I know you thought I had lost the plot when I spoke about my Angels but you always humoured me. You supported me by buying me an iPad (twice after breaking the first one) and a computer to write my book, because you had faith in me.

Thank you for putting up with me for two years, tap, tap, tapping on my computer, iPad and phone. I know the bright light in your face every night must have been annoying, I appreciate you covering your face with the duvet! Also, Thank you for sleeping in the spare room when I needed to rustle through papers to do my editing.

Thank you for moaning at me, being harsh and critical when reading my book. If it wasn't for you I would not have pushed myself to write this book and show you I could do it, when you said I couldn't. Well I've done it! No more sleeping in the spare room for a while! Love you so much.

Aileen Dunlop (GodMother), Natasha Casey (God-Daughter), Becky Nanda (Sister in Law), Bonny Mayorga (Sister) and Manisha Sethi (Cousin) - Thank you for doing the most tedious, hardest and mind numbing job of all - editing my book on several occasions. Also for reading many drafts and giving me constructive criticism and feedback. I am so grateful for the time you put in to make my dreams a reality. I owe you all a nice cold bottle of Prosecco!

Hayley Bray (my Bestfriend known as Hayley McBrayley) - Thank you for editing the first draft of my book. Even though I didn't receive it back as it got lost in the post! Still to this day, I have not received it, I wonder where it could be? Even though I didn't receive it, I can only imagine the time you would have put in to reading and editing it. I can't believe I didn't have the pleasure of seeing your green pen and your teacher style crossing out. Once again Thank you and next time I am to receive something, please hand deliver it!

Naresh Bassi (Dad), Ashish Kohli (Uncle), Archana Kohli (Aunty), Phil Heeley and Djamila Vogelsperger (Wise Friends) - For being there when I needed it the most. You were my role models who taught me life skills to grow and blossom to the person I am. You put me on the right path, helped, guided, supported, comforted me and kicked my ass so very lovingly if I ever fell off track. You gave me a home to live in and cared for me as if I was your own (bar my Dad, I am your own). You gave me hope and faith in times of despair and were there for me at the lowest points in my life.

You picked me up and lifted me high, reminding me of who I was. The love you gave me was unconditional and the wisdom you shared helped me to write this book. I want to make you proud and I hope you are. I wouldn't be here today if it was not for you. You were my foundation at the beginning of my awakening and journey and always will be.

Nanimama (Nan) - Thank you to my Nan, who listened to my dreams of writing a book for many years. I'll never forget the tuts, sighs and rolling of the eyes when I would visualise and communicate my dreams to you.

Thanks for putting up with me talking about my Angels and numbers and humouring me. You never said I was crazy, but your facial expressions said it all. You I am afraid to say, wouldn't make a good actress. Sorry Queenie! I still love you and the food you made me when I used to live with you. Thank you for giving me your room so I felt at home and looking after me.

I don't think, you believed me when I said I was going to write a book. I don't blame you. I never really stick at anything for this long. You said you will believe it when you see it, well I hope you have your glasses on and are reading this now! I did it.

Niraj Nanda - To my Brother in Law, Thank you for producing my front cover for this book. Your creative, wizardry abilities on the computer never cease to amaze me. Also, thank you for giving me your time (I know you are a very busy man!)

Jose Mayorga - To my Brother in Law, Thank you for all the advertising material you produced to help me get my book out there. Thank you for also helping me with the spine and back cover of my book. Also, I would like to thank you for helping me interpret and write in Spanish to other people in Spain who wanted to discuss 11:11. You helped me to reach out to other people. I would not have been able to do so, if it wasn't for you, Gracias.

Natasha Mwamba, Hayley Bray, Vicky Merrick and Lauren Heeley - Thank you to my four Best friends for being my kindred spirits, making me laugh, smile and find the real me. You brought so much joy and curiosity into my life. With you all the magic in the world occurred and without you my world would be sad. Thanks for supporting me on my journey and just being on the other end of the phone or a pen to give me words of wisdom. Also thanks for kicking me up the butt and telling me how things were when I needed it the most.

My Beautiful Baby Boy Rishi G Nanda - Baby, this one is especially for you. You are almost two years old. You were my motivation to finish this book. I am a full time Mummy and looking after you is a full time privilege.

After a hard day, cooking, cleaning, changing your nappies, winding, feeding, changing, bathing, playing, taking you out and doing the food shop; I was sometimes too tired to write. But when I looked at you sleeping, it would give me the energy, determination and motivation to write.

I wanted you to be proud of me when you were older. To say your Mummy wrote a book and stayed up until 3am some nights just to finish it. And she did it for you!! I want you to know that you can do anything if you put your mind to it. All you have to do is set your intentions and Do it. Always remember: Believe in yourself even when others doubt you. Have faith in your abilities and never be afraid to ask for help. Dream big, the sky is your limit!

You taught me what true love is. I will love you forever - unconditionally xx

Stephen Baker Ebook by Design – Thank you for converting my ebook/book and answering hundreds of questions I had for you. The time, effort and prompt replies helped me to complete my project. You gave me support, guidance and made me feel at ease and trust you with completing something that means a lot to me. Your professionalism and knowledge was astounding. I look forward to working with you in the future and would definitely recommend you.

11:11 Friends and Associates - Thank you to those who allowed me to share their personal experiences and for blessing and gracing me with many conversations: **Uri Gellar, Mary Jac, Jaycee, Maria, Kim Szuta, Juthy, Greg Doniger, Andrea Jen, Kammilah,, Lexus, Eric Youngren and Julie Ann.**

I would also like to Thank those who shared their social media details to help others in this experience. These are the 11:11 Kings, Queens and Gurus that made up my 11:11 team for the ending of this book, but the beginning of other peoples' journeys. It is with sincere gratitude to you all: **Julie Ann, Steve, Solara, Cassidy Cayne, Sarah Cherry and Georgina Beament.**

Julie Ann (The founder of Global Vision) - Thank you for taking me under your wing when I first came onto

Twitter and Facebook. Thank you for being so lovely and helpful, especially towards the end of my publication. You supported me, directed me and gave me positive feedback, which motivated me and put a smile on my face. You my dear friend are an inspiration and I would like to say thank you with all my heart for connecting with me. I send you much love and heartfelt blessings.

To all my Twitter and Facebook followers and fans - Thank you for all the retweets, favourites, comments, emails, messages, likes and shares. You helped me spread the message and find other people who are experiencing this phenomenon so they no longer feel alone. I have had many lengthy conversations about 11:11 leading on to other discussions. I was able to help others as they trusted me and also learned a lot on my way. This book is dedicated to you all.

You the reader - Thank you for taking the time to read this book. I hope that I have touched your heart, made you think and opened up a doorway for you to walk forward. Even if you only took one thing from this book, my purpose will have been fulfilled. Much love and blessings xxx

"11:11 is just the start
It's magical and wonderful
And has a place in my heart.
It communicates with me
This really is an art.

11:11 is my muse
With it by my side
I can never lose.
It helps me, guides me and shows me the way,
I see it almost every day.

11:11 is my guide
It takes me on a journey
Where I can find.
All I have to do it follow my mind.

11:11 is my friend
Sometimes it drives me loopy
And around the bend.
But it prevailed
In the end."

Natasha Nanda

Made in the USA
Charleston, SC
22 February 2017